SCIENCE
ESSENTIALS
PHYSICS

The Solar System and Beyond

GERARD CHESHIRE

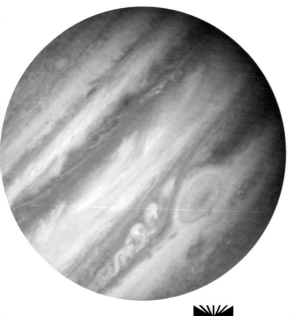

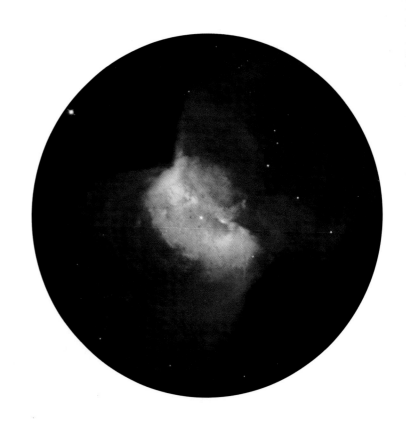

Evans

EVANS

LONDON

© Evans Brothers Ltd 2006

Published by:
Evans Brothers
2a Portman Mansions
Chiltern Street
London W1U 6NR

Series editor:
Harriet Brown

Editor:
Harriet Brown

Design:
Robert Walster

Illustrations:
Q2A Creative

Printed in China by
WKT Company Limited

British Library Cataloguing in
Publication Data

 Cheshire, Gerard, 1965-
   The solar system and beyond. -
(Science essentials.
   Physics)
   1.Astronomy - Juvenile literature
2.Solar system - Juvenile
   literature
   I.Title
   523.2

ISBN-10: 0237530066
13-digit ISBN (from 1 January 2007)
978 0 23753006 8

Contents

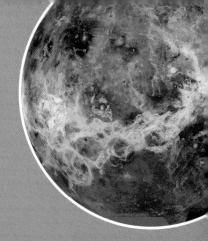

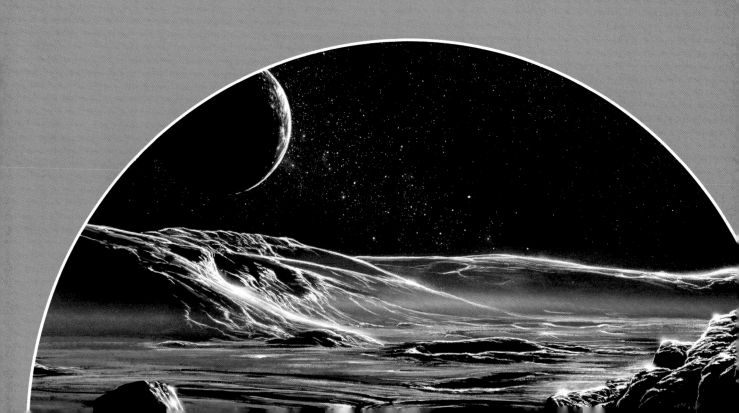

Introduction

We often take our planet for granted, and we rarely think about our place in the Solar System and the Universe. Planet Earth inhabits a tiny portion of space and is surrounded by other planets, moons, stars and galaxies.

This book takes you on a journey to learn more about our planet, the Solar System, and beyond into outer space. Find out why earthquakes and tsunamis happen on Earth, learn about the conditions on other planets, and get to grips with the vast distances between us and the stars. You can also find out about the famous scientists who uncovered some of the secrets of our Solar System, take a closer look at how scientists think the Universe began, and consider whether we are alone in the Universe.

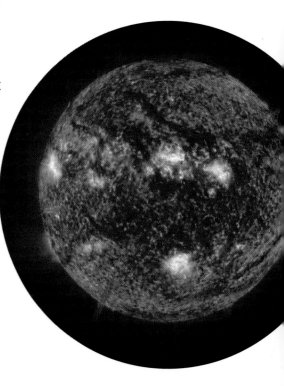

This book also contains feature boxes that will help you to unravel more about the mysteries of the Universe. Test yourself on what you have learnt so far; investigate some of the concepts discussed; find out more key facts; discover some of the scientific findings of the past and see how these might be utilised in the future.

DID YOU KNOW?

▶ Watch out for these boxes – they contain surprising and fascinating facts about the Solar System and beyond.

TEST YOURSELF

▶ Use these boxes to see how much you've learnt. Try to answer the questions without looking at the book, but take a look if you are really stuck.

INVESTIGATE

▶ These boxes contain experiments that you can carry out at home. The equipment you will need is usually cheap and easy to find.

TIME TRAVEL

▶ These boxes describe scientific discoveries from the past, and fascinating developments that pave the way for the advance of science in the future.

ANSWERS

At the end of this book on page 46, you will find the answers to questions from the 'Test yourself' and 'Investigate' boxes.

GLOSSARY

Words highlighted in **bold** are described in detail in the glossary on pages 46 and 47.

Planet Earth, inside and out

Planet Earth is truly remarkable yet we take it for granted because it is our home. It has all of the ingredients necessary for life, such as moderate temperatures, water and oxygen. It supports billions of organisms, from microscopic bacteria to vast blue whales, and intelligent life forms, such as man. Earth is the only planet that we know about that supports life.

HOW OLD IS EARTH?

Scientific evidence suggests that planet Earth is around 4.6 billion years old. Life is thought to have first appeared roughly 3.6 billion years ago. The first humans did not **evolve** until around four million years ago, and *Homo sapiens* (modern day humans) have only been around for 35,000 years. Life on Earth is about a million times older than our own species.

HOW DID PLANET EARTH FORM?

Scientists do not know for certain how planet Earth formed. The most widely believed theory is that it began as a spinning cloud of matter - **atoms** and **molecules**. Eventually the matter may have compressed (squashed) into a spinning sphere and then layered itself depending on its **mass**. The heaviest matter formed the centre and the lightest formed the edge of the sphere. This formed the basic structure of the planet. Over millions of years, planet Earth collected a great deal of extra matter, as debris from space collided with it.

THE EARTH TODAY

At the centre of the Earth is a solid iron core. Surrounding the core is a fluid layer of molten rock, called **magma**. The magma forms the mantle, which is divided into an upper and lower level. Planet Earth's surface is described as a crust because it is a solid layer floating on top of an ocean of fluid magma. The crust is cool and hard, and varies in thickness across the globe. Under the oceans, the crust is relatively thin, around five kilometres thick, whereas under the continents, such as the Americas or Europe, the crust can be up to 65 kilometres thick. The crust and topmost part of the upper mantle form the **lithosphere**.

▲ Planet Earth

Planet Earth's crust has remained roughly the same thickness for billions of years. It is made up of sections known as tectonic plates, which sit together like a badly-fitting jigsaw. The molten layer under the crust constantly moves as hot magma rises and cool magma sinks. This creates currents, which move around the lithosphere (plates and topmost part of the upper mantle). In some places, the plates push together and bend or crumple; in other places the edge of one plate lies over the edge of another. The plates can rub and snag against one another. It is this process of plate movement that is known as plate tectonics.

The plate tectonic process happens very slowly and on a very large scale, so we don't usually notice it. However, it moves the landmasses of the Earth by a few centimetres every year. This is called 'continental drift'. Where landmasses have collided, hills and mountain ranges have formed. Where landmasses have divided, rift valleys and oceans have formed. Although these features have developed over a very long period of time, plate tectonics have some dramatic short-term effects, too.

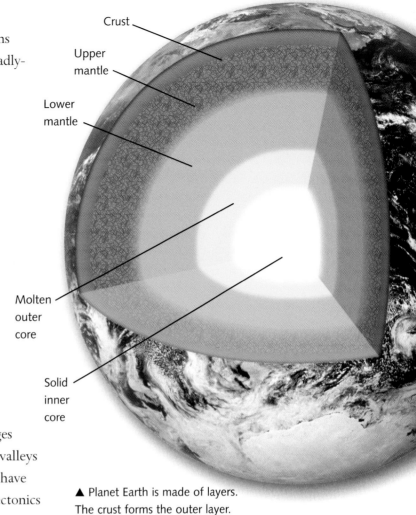

▲ Planet Earth is made of layers. The crust forms the outer layer.

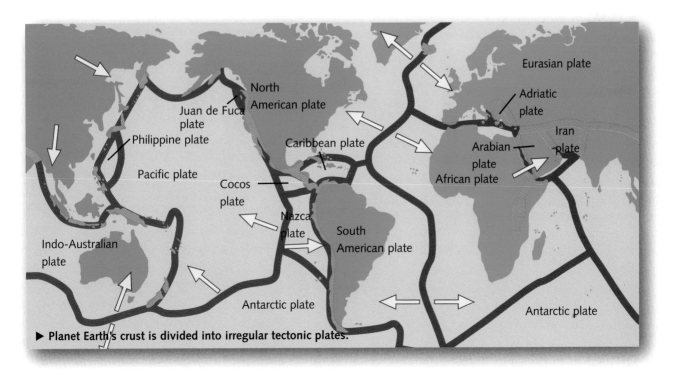

▶ Planet Earth's crust is divided into irregular tectonic plates.

VOLCANOES, EARTHQUAKES AND TSUNAMIS

You are likely to have seen reports of volcanoes, earthquakes and tsunamis on the news. These events are caused by plate tectonics and always occur where two plates meet each other. These areas are called **fault lines**.

Earthquakes – The movement of one plate against another is rarely smooth. Instead, they push against each other causing the pressure to build up. Eventually, the plates suddenly move. This movement is an earthquake. The energy released by the earthquake can have devastating effects, destroying buildings and claiming many lives. The San Andreas fault line in California, USA, is the site of regular earthquakes. Over the last three million years, the rate of motion of the plates has been 5.6 centimetres per year. This is roughly the same rate at which your fingernails grow. If the plates carry on moving at the same rate, Los Angeles and San Francisco, which today are roughly 600 kilometres apart, will be next to one another in approximately 15 million years.

Tsunamis – If an earthquake happens under the sea or ocean, the movement of the plates creates a massive wave called a tsunami. On the 26th December, 2004, a tsunami was generated off the coast of Sumatra in the Indian Ocean. The plates are thought to have shifted by up to 30 metres, which released as much energy as 23,000 atomic bombs. The tsunami spread out thousands of kilometres across the ocean at the speed of an aeroplane. It reached and swept over large areas of land killing over 240,000 people in 13 countries.

▲ This is the most visible part of the San Andreas fault line.

▼ The 2004 tsunami hit Thailand with incredible force.

▲ One of Mount Etna's many eruptions lasted 406 days.

Volcanoes – A volcano is a hill or mountain that has been formed by molten rock that has spewed from its opening. Volcanoes only form along fault lines where the crust is weak enough to allow magma to reach the surface. Volcanoes erupt when the pressure of the magma builds up underneath the crust and becomes great enough to propel itself from the top of the volcano. When magma reaches the surface of a volcano it is called **lava**. Mount Etna, in Italy, is one of the world's most active volcanoes. It has been erupting periodically for thousands of years.

DID YOU KNOW?

▶ A number of islands are known as volcanic islands, because they are actually made from the lava spewed out by underwater volcanoes. The Hawaiian Islands are arranged in a line. They have been made by the same volcano erupting at different times. The position of the volcano has changed as the tectonic plate has moved.

▶ Iceland is the world's largest volcanic island.

▶ Volcanic eruptions are so violent that they can throw hot rocks over 30 kilometres. They spew ash and fumes into the atmosphere, which can spread for 160 kilometres or more. Eruptions have been known to knock down entire forests, and trigger tsunamis, flash floods, earthquakes, mudslides, rock-falls and avalanches. People that live near a volcano must be ready to evacuate their homes at a moment's notice.

EARTH'S ATMOSPHERE

A layer of gases, called the atmosphere, surrounds planet Earth. The mixture of gases includes 78 per cent nitrogen, 21 per cent oxygen, and trace amounts of other gases, such as carbon dioxide and argon. The atmosphere protects life on Earth from the most harmful rays of the Sun. It also reduces the temperature extremes between day and night by preventing some rays from reaching planet Earth during the day, and by retaining warmth at night. The atmosphere gradually becomes thinner as you move further and further from the Earth's surface. Three-quarters of the Earth's atmosphere is within 11 kilometres of its surface. There is no cut-off point between the atmosphere and 'space', although people that travel beyond 80 kilometres from the Earth are said to be astronauts.

▲ The eye of a hurricane (see page 11) contains relatively calm weather. The wind swirling around the eye is extremely violent.

WEATHER

The Sun heats the Earth's surface unevenly, because the surface is irregular and the planet is always spinning on its axis (see pages 12-13). This means that some pockets of air become warmer than others. The warmer pockets rise, while the cooler pockets sink. This creates currents of air, which are also known as wind.

The atmosphere also contains water vapour that has evaporated (turned from a liquid into a gas) from the waterways of the world. When the water vapour cools in the atmosphere it condenses (turns from a gas into a liquid) and forms clouds. Eventually the air cannot contain any more water vapour and the water droplets fall to the Earth as rain, snow or hail. This water cycle then begins all over again.

Parts of planet Earth are subject to extreme forms of weather, such as hurricanes, tornadoes and thunderstorms. Hurricanes, also known as tropical cyclones or typhoons, are massive areas of swirling clouds, wind, torrential rain and thunderstorms. The winds in a hurricane are incredibly forceful, over 117 kilometres per hour, and destroy buildings, rip up trees and generate massive waves at sea.

DAY AND NIGHT

Planet Earth is situated 150 million kilometres from the Sun. Every day, the Sun appears to move across the sky from east to west. In fact, the Sun does not move. The Earth is still spinning on its axis, like a spinning top, just as it was when it formed billions of years ago. It spins once every 24 hours and as it does so, different parts of the Earth are exposed to light and heat from the Sun – one half of planet Earth is always lit by the Sun and one half is in shadow. This is why we have day and night.

During the night, the stars appear to move across the sky in the same way as the Sun appears to move during the day. The stars are not moving at all; the Earth's rotation causes the illusion.

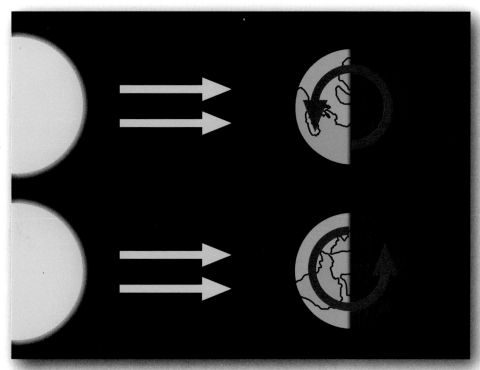

◄ This diagram shows the Sun and the Earth as though you are looking down on the 'top' of the Sun and down on the North Pole of the Earth. We have day and night because the Earth is spinning. As the Earth spins, different parts of it are exposed to sunlight.

THE SEASONS

Planet Earth is divided into two regions, the Northern Hemisphere and the Southern Hemisphere. The imaginary line around the centre of Earth is the Equator. The Earth travels around the Sun in an **orbit**. It takes roughly 365 days for it to travel once around the Sun. During the 365-day year, the seasons change. This happens because the Earth is tilted on its axis at an angle of 23.5°.

So, at any one time during summer or winter, one part of the planet is more directly exposed to the rays of the Sun. When the Northern Hemisphere is tilted towards the Sun, it is more directly exposed to the Sun and experiences summer. At the same time, the Southern Hemisphere is tilted away from the Sun and experiences winter. This is why when Europe and North America have summer, Australia has winter, and vice versa. At the Equator there is very little difference in the seasons because it always receives a lot of strong and direct sunshine. At the North and South Poles, there is a dramatic difference in summer and winter. The Poles have almost no sunshine during their winter, but during the summer, the Sun barely sets at all.

The number of hours of sunlight experienced each day also changes with the seasons. Again, the tilt of Earth is such that places experiencing summer are exposed to the Sun for more hours each day than those experiencing winter.

▼ Planet Earth is tilted on its axis. Here we can see how the Earth's orbit causes the seasons. In the diagram, the Northern Hemisphere of the Earth on the left is experiencing summer. The Southern Hemisphere of the Earth on the right is experiencing summer.

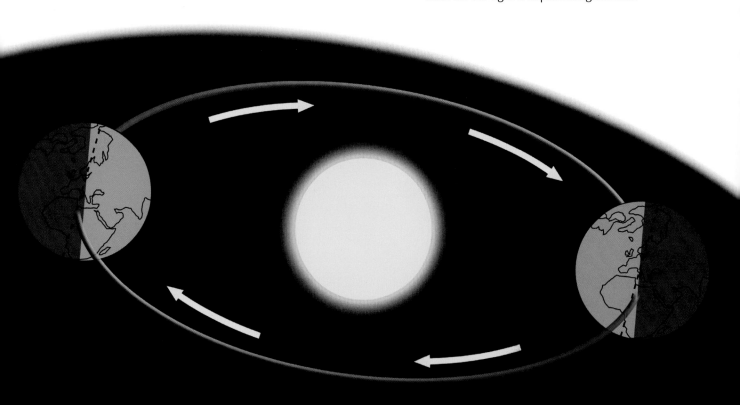

▶ Compared with other planets, temperatures on planet Earth are relatively constant. However, on 13th September 1922, a record temperature of 58°C was recorded in Libya. At this temperature you could fry an egg on the pavement.

▶ On 21st July 1983, a record low temperature of -89.2°C was recorded in Antarctica. At this temperature, which is colder than your freezer, your breath would freeze instantly into ice crystals and a thick layer of ice would form in the fine hair around your nostrils and mouth.

▶ **In extremely cold weather, ice forms on any exposed hairs.**

LEAP YEARS

Planet Earth actually takes 365.25 days to orbit the Sun. We save up the extra quarters until we have enough to make up a full day. Then, every four years, we have a leap year, which has 366 days. The extra day falls on the 29th February.

▶ The air flowing around a hurricane spins anti-clockwise in the Northern Hemisphere, and clockwise in the Southern Hemisphere. The rotation of the Earth produces a force, called a Coriolis force. This controls the direction in which the hurricane rotates. Hurricane activity is greatest in late summer. This is because for a hurricane to form, the sea temperatures must be warm. Hurricanes almost always form close to the Equator because this is where the Coriolis force is strongest.

▶ The deadliest hurricane on record hit the densely populated Ganges Delta region of Bangladesh in 1970. It is believed to have killed between 200,000 to 500,000 people.

▶ One of the most powerful hurricanes to have hit land was Hurricane Camille in 1969. It had sustained winds of up to 305 kilometres per hour and gusts of up to 335 kilometres per hour. It caused devastation in Louisiana, Mississippi and Alabama, USA.

▶ The largest hurricane on record was Typhoon Tip, which developed in the northwestern Pacific Ocean in 1979. It was 2,170 kilometres wide.

Gravity and space

Planet Earth is held in its orbit around the Sun by the force of **gravity**. Without gravity, Earth would fly off into outer space and you would fly off the Earth. All objects have gravity. Gravity is a pulling force that an object exerts on other objects. Massive objects exert a greater gravitational pull than less massive objects. For example, the pull between you and your classmate is about 500 times smaller than the pull between you and the Earth.

GRAVITY AND SPACE

Compared to the Earth, the Sun is vast. If the Sun was the size of a basketball, Earth would be the size of the head of a pin. One million Earths could fit inside the Sun. Because the Sun has such a great mass, it exerts a very powerful gravitational pull on the Earth, and on the other planets in the Solar System (see pages 26-35). This pull keeps the planets in their orbits. The size of the Sun's gravitational pull depends on the distance between it and the planet, and on the mass of the planet. It pulls closer planets more strongly than distant planets and it pulls massive planets more strongly than small planets. Orbits are not usually perfect circles and most planets travel an elliptical orbit (oval shaped path) around the Sun.

BIG BANG THEORY

The **Big Bang** theory suggests that the **Universe** began with an enormous explosion. All energy and matter is believed to have started as a densely packed ball with nothing beyond, which then spontaneously exploded to create space and time. Gravity plays an important role in the Big Bang theory. After the explosion, the Universe was nothing more than a cloud of matter travelling through space. In time, the matter began to pull together due to forces of gravity. The clumps of matter grew into spheres and began to spin. As each sphere became denser they began to spin faster. Pieces of the spheres separated and evolved into the components of the Universe that exist today, such as the stars, planets and moons.

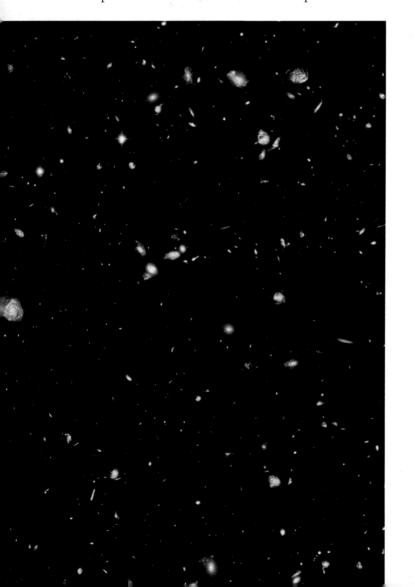

◄ Without the force of gravity, the early Universe would not have formed into separate bodies such as stars, planets and galaxies. Each of these oval shaped bodies is a vast galaxy.

SPACE

Space is the word we use to describe the void or vacuum between the bodies of our Solar System and everything beyond that makes up the Universe. It exists because gravity has caused the matter of the Universe to collect together into solar systems and **galaxies** (see pages 38-41). However, space is not completely empty. For example, when stars reach the end of their lives, some of them explode and send particles of matter flying through space.

DARK MATTER

Scientists use calculations to find out the distances of stars and galaxies from planet Earth, their mass and the directions in which they're moving. In recent years, they have discovered that some of their calculations do not add up as expected. Their observations tell them that there are

▲ This long narrow dust cloud is the Pencil Nebula. It formed when a star exploded at the end of its life.

different kinds of matter and energy in space that we cannot see or detect, even with highly specialised telescopes. They have called this matter 'dark matter' and the energy 'dark energy'. Very little is known about dark matter and dark energy. However, about 25 per cent of the Universe is thought to be composed of dark matter and 70 per cent is thought to consist of dark energy. So, scientists can only see around five per cent of all matter in the Universe!

TEST YOURSELF

▶ Explain why gravity is so important on Earth.

▶ Explain why gravity is important for our Solar System.

Moons and satellites

Just as the Earth orbits the Sun, the Moon orbits the Earth. Other planets are also orbited by moons. Moons are always smaller than their parent planets, but their size can vary widely. For example, the planet Pluto is smaller than the largest moon of the planet Jupiter. Although the Earth has just one moon, some planets have many moons. Jupiter has over 70 moons. Usually, moons are spherical in shape, but some have irregular shapes. A moon of Mars, called Phobos, looks similar to a potato. Any object that orbits another object is called its satellite.

PLANET EARTH'S MOON

The Earth's Moon may be seen day or night. It is the only natural satellite of the Earth and is estimated to be more than three billion years old. The Moon has virtually no atmosphere to protect it. Therefore, it is scarred by thousands of impact craters from **meteorites**, which have struck it and imbedded themselves in its surface.

The Moon is 3,476 kilometres wide, which makes it less than a third of the diameter of the Earth. It is less dense (compacted) than the Earth, and is made from many chemicals such as uranium, iron, calcium and hydrogen. Its overall mass is about 1.25 per cent of the Earth's, making it a relatively large moon. The Moon is on average 384,400 kilometres from the Earth, but during its orbit it can come as close as 351,000 kilometres because it follows an elliptical path.

From the Earth, our view of the Moon is always the same because the Moon spins on its axis at almost exactly the same rate as the Earth spins. It makes one full rotation every 27.3 days. The 'dark side of the Moon' is the side we never see, but it is only actually in darkness when we see a full Moon.

◄ The Moon has been struck by objects flying through space. This is why it is covered in craters. This image was taken by the crew of Apollo 10 in 1969.

DID YOU KNOW?

► When the sky is clear at night, the Moon can reflect so much light from the Sun that it is possible to see quite clearly. This is called moonshine. Occasionally, it is possible to see the portion of the Moon that is not directly lit by the Sun. This is because planet Earth reflects sunlight onto the Moon. This is called earthshine.

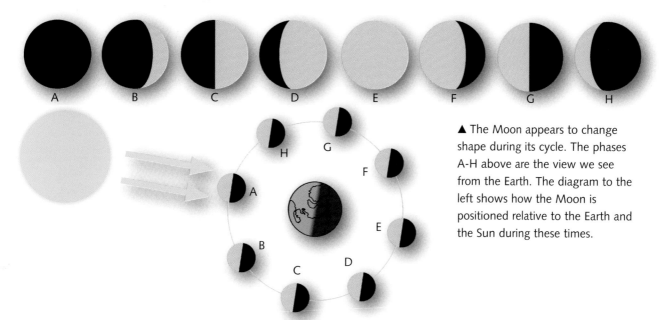

▲ The Moon appears to change shape during its cycle. The phases A–H above are the view we see from the Earth. The diagram to the left shows how the Moon is positioned relative to the Earth and the Sun during these times.

We are able to see the Moon because it is lit up by the Sun – it does not give out any of its own light. It appears to change shape because we see different amounts of its sunlit side from one day to the next. The Moon goes through phases throughout its cycle – full moon, half moon, waning crescent, new moon, waxing crescent, half moon, full moon – in a cycle lasting roughly one month.

THE MOON AND TIDES

The most important effect that the Moon has on the Earth is its gravitational pull as it passes above the surface. The Earth's gravity holds the Moon in orbit and holds its own surface in position. However, the gravity of the Moon attracts the Earth's surface. In places where there is land, the Moon's gravity has little effect, but in places where there is water it causes tides as the water is lifted in the direction of the Moon. You are likely to have noticed the high and low tides of the sea or ocean. The Moon actually causes the oceans to bulge on both sides of the globe at the same time. The bulge occurs on the opposite side of the Earth because the Earth itself is also being pulled toward the Moon and away from the water on the far side. There are two high tides and two low tides during the course of 24 hours, as Earth rotates on its axis.

There is also a slight shift in their times from one day to the next because the Moon's position changes as it orbits the Earth. The gravity of the Sun can also add to the pull of the Moon when they are positioned in a straight line. This causes spring tides twice a month. Spring tides are exceptionally high and low tides. In between the spring tides there are neap tides, where the least difference between high and low tides occurs.

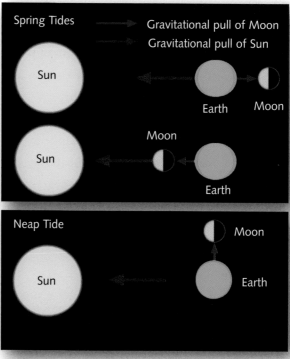

▲ The Moon's and the Sun's gravity pulls the Earth's oceans and seas. This causes the tides.

ECLIPSES

Eclipses occur when the Sun, the Earth and the Moon all line up exactly. If they are arranged Sun-Moon-Earth then the shadow of the Moon falls on the Earth – a solar eclipse. During a total solar eclipse, the Moon is directly in front of the Sun, and the Earth is plunged into darkness as though it were night time for about three minutes. It is important never to look directly at the Sun, at any time. A lunar eclipse happens when the three bodies arrange in a line in the order Moon-Earth-Sun. The Moon moves through the shadow cast by the Earth. This can only happen when there is a full Moon.

ASTEROIDS

There are a great many bodies orbiting the Sun that don't qualify as planets because they are too small. An **asteroid** is a medium-sized rocky or metallic object that orbits the Sun. The largest asteroids are larger than some moons. They are

▲ In this eclipse, the Moon is positioned between the Earth and the Sun. The Moon blocks the Sun's light and casts a shadow across the Earth. The bright area around the Sun is called the corona. It can only be seen clearly during an eclipse.

sometimes called minor planets or planetoids. There is one region, called the asteroid belt, within which most asteroids in our Solar System orbit the Sun. It lies between the orbits of Mars and Jupiter (see pages 26-35). The asteroid that comes nearest to the Earth is called Eros – it is a Near Earth asteroid and orbits the Sun between the orbits of Earth and Mars. Roughly every 46 years or so it comes within 24 million kilometres of our world, which in astronomical terms is too close for comfort. Although Eros does not cross the Earth's orbit, many asteroids have collided with the Earth and other planets. Eros is believed to be a fragment from an ancient collision, because it is shaped irregularly like a broken piece of a larger body.

Scientists calculate the orbits of asteroids and then work out whether they will cross the Earth's path. Eventually they obtain enough data to find out whether they will collide with the Earth. It is believed that the dinosaurs were made extinct by an asteroid impact around 65 million years ago.

COMETS

There are other bodies that independently orbit the Sun, called **comets**. Comets are made of ice, rock and carbon-based substances. They are thought to have come from other parts of the Universe and been caught by the Sun's gravity as they attempted to pass by. They have huge orbits that sweep far out into space and then come closer to the Sun as they travel around it. The most well-known comet is Halley's comet – named after Edmund Halley who observed it in 1682. Halley's comet is visible in the night sky every 76 years. It last appeared in 1986 and is due again in 2062. When comets approach the Sun they tend to display long tails. This is because layers of ice on the comet melt away, releasing gas and dust particles, which shoot away in a plume. The force of the Sun pushes against the tail and therefore, the tail always points away from the Sun. In 1994, a comet called Shoemaker Levy 9 crashed into the planet Jupiter. This was witnessed by **astronomers** across the globe, and was the first observed collision of two bodies in the Solar System. Thousands of kilometres of debris were thrown into space.

▼ The comet has two tails; a white dust tail and a blue ion tail. The dust tail is made of dust blown off the comet by sunlight. The ion tail is made up of glowing ionised gas pushed off the comet by the solar wind.

KUIPER BELT

The Kuiper belt is a field of debris made from icy, comet-like substances. It orbits the Sun outside the orbit of Neptune. The majority of the debris is between 10 and 50 kilometres in diameter, but at least 70,000 objects have a diameter greater than 100 kilometres.

METEOROIDS, METEORS AND METEORITES

As well as the larger satellites of the Sun – planets, moons, asteroids and comets – a great many smaller fragments of rock also orbit around it. These are called **meteoroids**. At certain times of the year and on clear nights you can see meteoroids collide with the Earth's atmosphere. When this happens, heat is generated which causes the meteoroids to glow and burn away. You may have seen 'shooting stars' on clear nights. These are meteoroids burning up in the Earth's atmosphere. When they are visible like this, they are called **meteors**.

Occasionally meteoroids are large enough to survive the journey through Earth's atmosphere, so that their hot cores reach the surface. These surviving fragments are called meteorites. Most meteorites are lost in the ground or in the oceans, but they are sometimes found on ice sheets or desert sands.

MAN-MADE SATELLITES

The very first artificial satellite of the Earth was called Sputnik 1. It was launched into orbit in 1957. It carried a radio transmitter and sent back test signals for three weeks. Sputnik 2 carried the first animal into orbit – a dog, named Laika, who sadly, was never to return to Earth.

▼ Meteors look like streaks of light crossing the night sky. They appear and disappear very quickly.

The first communications satellite was a US machine named Telstar, sent up in 1962. Today, satellites are used for communication, astronomy, surveillance, meteorology and mapping of the Earth's surface.

SPACE PROBES

Space probes are unmanned space vehicles sent to explore the Moon, the Sun, other planets and the space in between. The first, Explorer 1, was launched in 1958. Luna 2 was the first to reach the Moon, in 1959, while the Mariner 2 was the first to reach another planet – Venus – in 1962. Since then, a great many space probes have been sent to explore the Solar System. Some have orbited other planets to become artificial satellites, while others have landed or crashed on planetary surfaces or simply continued travelling into outer space. Voyager 1 is the farthest man-made object from Earth. It has been travelling through our Solar System for over 28 years collecting information on the planets and other space objects and sending it back to Earth. It is now travelling way out beyond the edge of our Solar System.

▼ Voyager 1 is now 14 billion kilometres from the Sun.

TEST YOURSELF

▶ Explain 'meteorites', 'meteoroids' and 'meteors'.
▶ Name two differences between comets and asteroids.

▲ The International Space Station (ISS) orbits the Earth. It is maintained by six space agencies from the USA, Europe, Russia, Japan, Brazil and Canada. Astronauts live and work on the ISS for up to 195 days at a time.

SPACE VEHICLES

Manned space vehicles have, so far, been used to carry humans into orbit around the Earth and to the Moon. Man set foot on the Moon for the first time in 1969. Space vehicles are described as modules, capsules, shuttles and space stations, depending on their purpose. They all act as life support vessels for humans, who would otherwise perish in the hostile environments of space. It seems likely that technology will eventually allow people to travel safely in space ships to Mars, and survive journeys lasting months or even years.

4

Sun and stars

The Sun is at the centre of our Solar System. The Sun is a star with a diameter of over 100 times that of our planet. Scientists believe that the Sun is about 4.7 billion years old. Despite having existed for such a long time it still has plenty of life left in it, and is likely to provide light and heat for twice as long again.

LIGHT AND HEAT

The Sun generates its light and heat by a process called **fusion**. In this process, hydrogen atoms are converted into helium. It is an 'exothermic' reaction, which means that it releases energy as heat. This energy escapes the Sun in the form of electromagnetic radiation – x-rays, ultraviolet light, visible light, infrared light (heat), and gamma rays. The Sun still contains 70 per cent hydrogen – 29 per cent of the Sun has already been converted to helium. The remaining one per cent is oxygen and carbon.

▼ The Sun is a burning ball of gas. It contains mainly hydrogen.

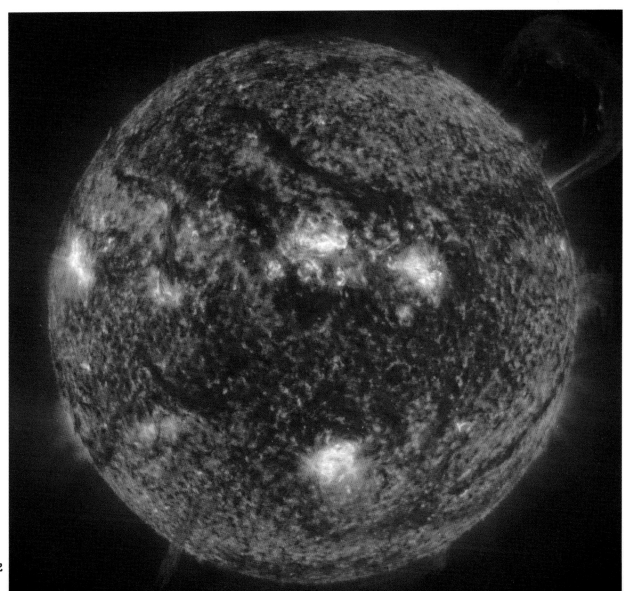

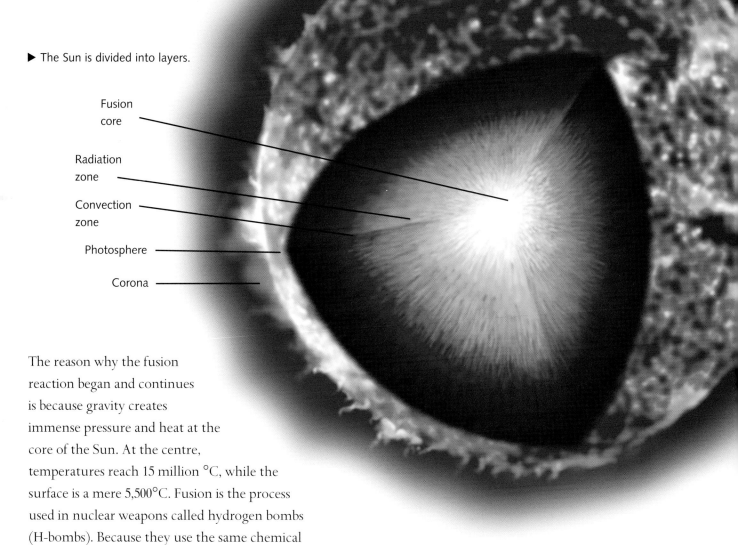

► The Sun is divided into layers.

Fusion core

Radiation zone

Convection zone

Photosphere

Corona

The reason why the fusion reaction began and continues is because gravity creates immense pressure and heat at the core of the Sun. At the centre, temperatures reach 15 million °C, while the surface is a mere 5,500°C. Fusion is the process used in nuclear weapons called hydrogen bombs (H-bombs). Because they use the same chemical reaction as the Sun, they produce extremely powerful explosions of electromagnetic radiation and nuclear radiation, which makes them very dangerous and frightening weapons.

STRUCTURE OF THE SUN

If the Sun were cut in half, you would see layers, similar to the layers of an onion. At the centre is the fusion core, where the fusion reaction takes place. It is surrounded by a radiation zone, and then by a convection zone. Radiation escapes from this area, and new fuel enters the core. Nearer the surface the photosphere is responsible for the light and yellowish colour emitted by the Sun. Finally there is an atmosphere-like outer skin called the corona, which is visible from Earth during total solar eclipses. The surface of the Sun is always in turmoil because of the violent currents produced by its energy. This is called solar activity. Using sun-viewing telescopes, scientists can see solar flares and sun spots where plumes of energy escape and die away again.

DID YOU KNOW?

► The Sun's corona produces a field of particles that escape the gravity of the Sun. This is called the solar wind.

► The solar wind is responsible for the aurora borealis and aurora australis – the northern and southern lights – where it collides with the Earth's atmosphere near the North and South Poles.

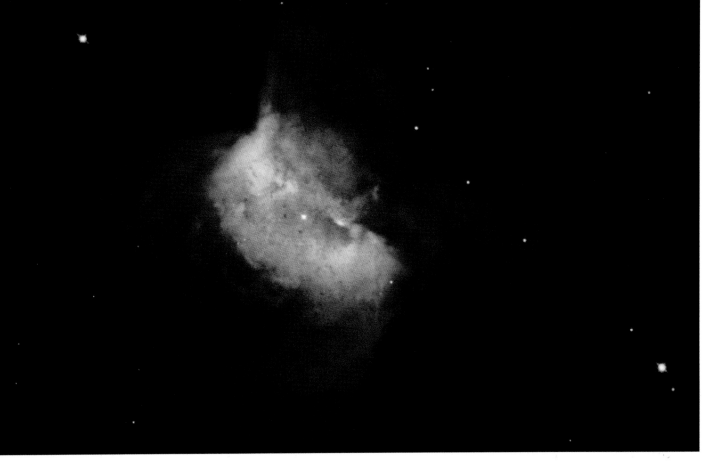

STARS

The Sun is just one of countless billions of stars throughout the Universe. As it is the star most familiar to us, we use it as a standard against which other stars can be measured. For example, our Sun is described as having one solar mass. Other stars can have up to 100 solar masses. As the Sun is comparatively small, and yellow in colour, it is classed as a 'yellow dwarf' star. It is a low mass star and over billions of years it will firstly expand massively to become a 'red giant' and will consume the planets closest to it – Mercury and possibly even Venus, too. It will then decrease in size to become a 'white dwarf' – about the size of Earth, but brighter. It will cool down and shrink further as it runs out of fuel, and eventually it will become a cold 'black dwarf' star – a cold, dark object. This may take billions or even trillions of years. Our Universe is too young to contain any black dwarf stars yet.

Larger stars are called giants and super giants. These stars suffer a different fate when they die. Instead of slowly cooling, they suddenly collapse under their own force of gravity, and result in a **supernova** explosion. Supernovae are among the most powerful explosions in the Universe and each one can release more than 100 times the energy our Sun will radiate over its entire 10 billion year lifetime. They can be brighter than an entire galaxy and radiate a vast cloud of matter in space called a '**nebula**'.

After the supernova, a giant star forms a tiny ball only around 10 kilometres in diameter, called a neutron star. Super giant stars collapse even further to form a mysterious tombstone called a black hole (see page 40).

Stars near and far

A **light year** is a unit of distance rather than time. One light year is the distance light travels in one year in space, which is approximately 9,460 billion kilometres. Our nearest star, apart from the Sun, is Proxima Centauri, which is 4.24 light-years away. It would take a jet aeroplane, travelling at 938 kilometres per hour, over 4.8 million years to travel from Earth to Proxima Centauri.

Proxima Centauri is an unusual star because it is part of a triple-star system. It orbits a binary (double) star called Alpha Centauri/Lambda Centauri. The three stars merge to the naked eye and appear as the third brightest 'star' in the sky. They can only be seen in the Southern Hemisphere.

Constellations

Throughout history, humans have grouped stars into constellations. A constellation is a group of stars that appear to be related to one another in a pattern. However, in three-dimensional space, most of the stars in a constellation are great

INVESTIGATE

▶ Look in library books or on the internet for star constellations. Try to learn one or two of them and the next time there is a clear night, see if you can spot your chosen constellation in the sky.

distances from each other. You may recognise some constellations, such as Orion, which is visible from almost all parts of the globe at particular times of the year.

Pole star

The North Star, which is also called Polaris, sits almost directly above the North Pole. In the Northern Hemisphere, the North Star can be used for navigation. Although its position is relatively constant, the North Star does appear to change its position extremely slowly because the Earth wobbles slightly on its axis. In 2012, it will be as close to true north as it can get, and will then begin wandering away again. In 12,000 years time, a star called Vega will be nearest to true north.

▲ Orion is one of the most famous star constellations. It is named after Orion, who is a hunter in Greek mythology. The three central stars are said to represent his belt.

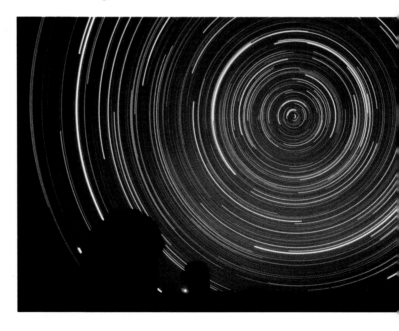

▲ In a time-lapse photo, the North Star appears to remain 'stationary' in the middle of the view. The other stars appear as lines because the Earth is rotating.

5

The Solar System

Our Solar System contains the Sun and all of the objects that orbit around it, including the planets, moons, asteroids, meteoroids and comets. It extends in all directions from the Sun to a distance where the Sun's gravitational pull can still influence objects orbiting it. So far, there are nine named planets in our Solar System – Mercury, Venus, Earth, Mars, Jupiter, Saturn, Uranus, Neptune and Pluto. And, in 2005, a tenth planet was discovered. If it is definitely a planet, it will be the furthest planet from the Sun in our Solar System. Its temporary name is 2003 UB 313. Planets vary dramatically in size, the substances from which they are made, and their distances from the Sun. Although some of the planets are huge in comparison to the Earth, they are all far smaller than the Sun.

Planet	Day length time taken to rotate once (number of Earth days)	Year length time taken to orbit the Sun once (number of Earth days)	Average distance from the Sun (million kilometres)	Max. day-time temperature (°C)	Min. night-time temperature (°C)
Mercury	176	88	58	+350	-170
Venus	243	225	108	+475	-40
Earth	1	365.26	150	+58	-89.2
Mars	1	687	228	+23	-85
Jupiter	0.41	4332	778	Surface temp -140	Core temp 20,000
Saturn	0.42	10750	1,429.39	Surface temp -180	Core temp 12,000
Uranus	0.71	30,707	2,870	Surface temp -214	
Neptune	0.66	60.202	4,497	Surface temp -220	
Pluto	6.4	90,803	5900	Surface temp -220	

▼ The planets of the Solar System vary widely in size. The Earth is the third planet from the right. (This diagram does not accurately show the distances between the planets.)

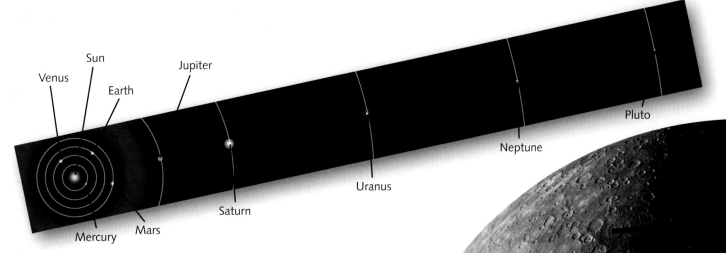

Venus
Sun
Earth
Jupiter

Mercury
Mars
Saturn
Uranus
Neptune
Pluto

▲ The inner planets are relatively close to one another. The outer planets are spaced much further apart.

MERCURY

Mercury is the planet closest to the Sun, and it orbits at an average distance of 58 million kilometres. It is a third of the size of the Earth, and the smallest of the four inner planets – Mercury, Venus, Earth and Mars. It can occasionally be seen with the naked eye, but only when it reflects the light of the Sun very brightly. The four inner planets are also called terrestrial planets because they are made from solid rock instead of gases and liquids.

Mercury has very little atmosphere. If you tried to land a spaceship on Mercury, the lack of atmosphere would mean that you would have a smooth approach. However, once there, there would be very little protection from asteroids. As a result, the surface of Mercury is littered with asteroid craters. Temperatures vary in the extreme on the surface of Mercury. During the day it is hot enough to melt zinc metal and during the night, it is almost cold enough to freeze argon (a gas found in the Earth's atmosphere).

▶ On Mercury, the Sun's light is 6.5 times more intense than it is here on Earth.

DID YOU KNOW?

▶ The planets in our Solar System can only be seen because they reflect sunlight. Venus reflects the most sunlight, and Pluto reflects the least.

▶ On Mercury, a day is longer than a year. It takes longer to rotate on its axis (176 Earth days) than it does to orbit the Sun (88 Earth days).

VENUS

Venus is often visible to the naked eye and at certain times of the year is the brightest object in the night sky – apart from the Moon. It is one of the least hospitable places in the Solar System. It has a very dense and poisonous atmosphere, which contains 96 per cent carbon dioxide and clouds of highly corrosive sulphuric acid. The crushing air pressure is equal to that found one kilometre below the oceans here on Earth. The surface temperature is hot enough to melt lead, and it has volcanoes 100 kilometres wide and five kilometres high. Although it is not as volcanically active now as it has been in the past, astronomers have discovered evidence of recent volcanic flows, and spreading and folding of the surface. Roughly twice a century, Venus passes directly between the Earth and the Sun. Seen through a filtered telescope, it appears as a black disc on the Sun's surface for a few minutes. This is called the transit of Venus and is due to happen again on June 5th 2012.

▲ Venus is roughly the same size as the Earth.

MARS

Mars is often called the red planet because its surface contains iron, which gives it a reddish-brown colour. It is thought to be the planet most like Earth and the most likely to have other forms of life, such as ancient bacteria (see pages 44-45). Mars has water on its surface at its poles, but it is frozen into ice. The atmosphere is 95 per cent carbon dioxide and quite thin with only traces of oxygen. Mars has two small moons, named Phobos and Deimos. The weather on Mars can be pleasant and similar in temperature to a warm summer's day on Earth. However, it is also extremely unpredictable. Massive storms can sweep across the whole planet, whipping up the red dust into tornadoes eight kilometres high, and causing the temperature to drop by 20 degrees in a matter of days.

▲ The white areas are Mars' polar ice caps.

DID YOU KNOW?

▶ The international scientific community hope to set up a manned base on Mars before the end of this century. They hope to manufacture oxygen from water and build biospheres on the surface of the planet, which would be made suitable for living and growing food.

JUPITER

Jupiter is the first of the four Jovian planets – Jupiter, Saturn, Uranus, Neptune – so called because they are all Jupiter-like. They are all massive planets made of liquids and gases, rather than solid matter like the terrestrial planets. Jupiter is the largest planet in our Solar System. It is bigger than the other eight planets put together and its diameter is 11 times that of Earth. It exerts an incredible gravitational pull on anything that comes near it. Despite its gigantic size, Jupiter has the shortest day of all the planets, spinning on its axis in just under 10 hours.

Jupiter is a swirling ball of colourful clouds and can often be seen in the night sky with the naked eye. Its atmosphere contains ammonia, hydrogen-sulphide and other chemicals and surrounds a universal ocean of liquid hydrogen. Next there is a layer of metallic hydrogen and at the centre is a rocky core.

The planet's most distinctive feature is its famous Great Red Spot, which is thought to be a storm, larger in diameter than Earth, which has been raging for at least 300 years.

No-one knows why this storm has lasted for so long. Probes have been sent to Jupiter but none have survived more than 150 metres into its atmosphere. Jupiter has sixteen named moons and dozens of smaller, unnamed moons that form a faint ring around its equator.

▼ Jupiter's Great Red Spot can be seen in the bottom left of this photograph.

SATURN

Saturn is the most distinctive planet in our Solar System, because it is surrounded by clearly visible rings. Although from a distance the rings look solid, they are actually made of billions of separate chunks of rock and ice. They range from microscopic pieces, to boulders several metres in diameter. Nobody is certain how or why the rings formed, but a likely theory is that they may have formed from larger moons that were shattered by comets or asteroids.

Like Jupiter, Saturn is made almost entirely of liquid hydrogen. However, it does not have a heavy core and its density is less than that of water. Saturn would float on water – if you could find a bath large enough. Saturn is an extremely windy planet. Around the equator, winds can reach an incredible 1,500 kilometres per hour. No probe has ever penetrated Saturn's surface, but in 2004, the unmanned Cassini spacecraft arrived at Saturn and dropped a probe onto one of Saturn's ten moons, Titan. The probe, called Huygens, travelled safely all the way to Titan's surface and sent photos and information back to Earth. Huygens found that the surface of Titan is very much like that of Earth's – it seems to have volcanoes, methane rain and rain clouds, stream-like channels and dry lake beds.

▼ Saturn bulges around its equator. This is because it spins rapidly and is a fluid planet.

DID YOU KNOW?

▶ Next time there is a clear night, look carefully at the sky, well away from any street lights. Notice how stars twinkle in the sky. Next, see if you can spot any that don't twinkle. Why do some 'stars' not twinkle?

▶ If you see a star in the night sky that does not twinkle, it is likely to be a planet. Through a telescope, a star looks like a single point of light, whereas a planet looks like a disc of light. When light travels through the Earth's atmosphere, it can wobble. When a single light point wobbles, it makes the star look as though it is twinkling. Light from a planet appears to come from a wider area, and although the light is still affected by the Earth's atmosphere, because there are many points of light joined together, the planet does not twinkle. So, even though planets are smaller than stars, planets don't twinkle because they are much closer than stars.

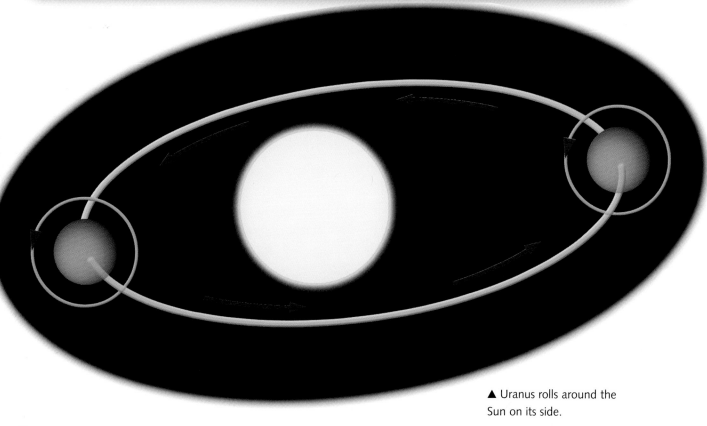

▲ Uranus rolls around the Sun on its side.

URANUS

Uranus has methane in its atmosphere, which gives it a greenish colour. It is thought to have a core of rock and ice surrounded by an atmosphere of hydrogen. It has over 21 moons and is four times bigger than the Earth. Uranus has other smaller satellites and a faint ring system. It appears to lie on its side and it spins in the same direction as it travels – it rolls around its orbit around the Sun. This means that each of Uranus' poles faces away from the Sun for half of the planet's orbit, and experiences 42-year nights and days. No-one knows why Uranus is the only planet in the Solar System to orbit on its side in this way. Uranus also has a ring system, but the debris that forms it is so dark that it cannot be seen directly. The only way to spot the rings is when they block out the light from the stars beyond. Uranus can occasionally be seen with the naked eye, although it is very faint.

NEPTUNE

Neptune is the eighth planet from the Sun. However, Pluto, the ninth planet does sometimes come closer to the Sun, because it follows an elliptical and off-centre orbit. The two planets have the potential to cross paths and collide when they are the same distance from the Sun. Fortunately, their orbits are on such a large scale, and take so long, that it is unlikely to happen during the entire life of the Sun and the Solar System.

Astronomers found Neptune soon after the discovery of Uranus. Neptune's gravitational pull affects the movement of Uranus. This 'wobble' of Uranus led the astronomers to search for another planet, which they found in 1846. Neptune is thought to be similar in structure to Uranus – having a solid core, surrounded by liquid gases.

It also has a ring system and over 11 moons. Neptune takes so long to orbit the Sun that it only does so six times every 1,000 years. Neptune has even fiercer winds than Saturn. They blow at over 2,000 kilometres per hour.

◀ Neptune is a cold and distant planet.

DID YOU KNOW?

▶ There is no precise scientific definition of the word 'planet'. Because of this, astronomers argue over whether or not Pluto and two new discoveries are planets. These newly found rocky bodies are called Sedna and Quaoar (pronounced 'kwah-whar'). Sedna was discovered in 2003 and is about two-thirds the size of Pluto. It orbits the Sun at over three times the distance of Pluto. If you stood on Sedna, you could block the entire Sun with the head of a pin held at arm's length. Quaoar was discovered in 2002 and is half the size of Pluto. It orbits the Sun in the Kuiper belt and its orbit crosses that of Pluto.

Pluto

Pluto is very dark, icy, extremely distant from the Sun, and remains largely a mystery. It is roughly one-fifth the size of the Earth and is so cold that in the winter, even the atmosphere freezes. Pluto has one moon, Charon. If you were to stand on Pluto, you could only see Charon from one side of the planet because Pluto spins at the same rate as Charon's orbit. Pluto is so small that some astronomers feel that it should be classed as a planetoid or asteroid. Like the four terrestrial planets, Pluto is made from solid, rocky materials. Astronomers used to think that Pluto was once

Test yourself

▶ Try to memorise the nine planets and repeat them in the correct order.

one of Neptune's moons, but was sent off on its own orbit by a collision with another of Neptune's moons, Triton, rather like an impact between snooker balls. This theory has become less popular, and others now believe that Triton used to have its own orbit around the Sun, but was captured by Neptune's gravity.

▲ An artist's impression of Charon, viewed from Pluto.

Many of the planets, such as Mercury, Venus, Mars, Jupiter and Saturn were observed by ancient civilisations. However, they did not understand the planets in a scientific way. It has only been in the last 500 years that we have begun to understand our place in the Solar System. Today, we take it for granted that the Sun is at the centre of the Solar System. We also accept that in astronomical terms, life-forms on Earth are very tiny and have only existed for the blink of an eye.

WHO DISCOVERED THAT EARTH ORBITS THE SUN?

In 1514, the Polish astronomer Nicolaus Copernicus wrote down his theory that the Sun was at the centre of the planetary system. At the time, everyone believed that the Earth was at the centre of the Universe, and the Sun and the other planets orbited around us. Copernicus lived at a very religious time when it was dangerous to suggest that humanity was not the most important thing in the Universe. He did not publish his idea until almost 30 years later in 1543, the year of his death. It caused a storm of controversy across Europe. Eventually, Copernicus' theory had to be accepted because mathematical calculations proved it to be undeniably true. Copernicus was responsible for the idea of a 'solar system' and religions had to accept that humanity was not at the centre of all creation.

THE UNIVERSE

The idea that the Solar System exists within a larger, universal space or Universe came in 1576 from Thomas Digges, an English astronomer. In England it was quite safe to write about the Solar System and the Universe, because King Henry VIII had replaced the Catholic Church with the Protestant Church, which was more open to scientific ideas. However, in continental Europe the Catholic Church was more opposed to such contentious ideas. Astronomers and scientists had to be careful about expressing their thoughts.

In 1600, an Italian scientist called Giordano Bruno was burned at the stake for expressing his belief in the Solar System and Universe. Galileo Galilei, an important mathematician and astronomer, also supported Copernicus' ideas. He was forced by the Catholic Church to deny his belief in a Solar System and lived under house arrest for the last 10 years of his life, for fear of execution.

INFLUENCE OF THE TELESCOPE

People's understanding of the Solar System grew with the invention of the telescope in 1576. The telescope used by Galilei had a magnification of about 30 and was good enough to make general observations of the planets.

In 1668, the English scientist Isaac Newton invented a telescope that worked by using a mirror and lens that captured and focussed on an image. The magnification of this telescope was much better and allowed astronomers to observe the

◄ **Copernicus changed the popular view of the Universe.**

Solar System in far more detail. The Italian astronomer Giovanni Domenico Cassini was able to calculate the orbiting distances of the planets, including Earth, in 1671. Between 1781 and 1930, Uranus, Neptune and Pluto were discovered (see pages 31-33).

Today, with the use of advanced telescopes, astronomers are still discovering new moons, large asteroids and planetoids, and are mapping and recording space objects. The Sloan Digital Sky Survey aims to map one-quarter of the night sky using its wide-angled 2.5 metre telescope. Space-based telescopes, such as Hubble, look even further into space in an attempt to unlock more of the Universe's well-kept secrets.

▲ Newton used this reflecting telescope to study the stars. Today, reflecting telescopes are popular with amateur astronomers because they are relatively cheap and simple to use.

▶ This telescope in New Mexico, USA, is part of the Sloan Digital Sky Survey, which aims to map more than 100 million space objects.

6

Secrets of the Universe

All that we know about the Universe has been discovered through the use of telescopes. Some telescopes detect light, and some detect other forms of radiation, such as radio waves, infrared radiation (heat) and ultraviolet light. Computers display this information on a screen so that humans can try to make sense of it. Thanks to our continually advancing technology, new discoveries are made and old theories are replaced by new. Our knowledge of the Universe is changing all the time.

LOOKING INTO THE UNIVERSE

All of the information that comes to the Earth from the Universe, comes in the form of radiation. All radiation travels at the speed of light through space. The information received on Earth, or from a satellite telescope, is never brand new. For example, our nearest star, Proxima Centauri, is 4.24 light years away (see page 25), so the radiation received is already 4.24 years old when it arrives at Earth. In other words, astronomers always see or detect Proxima Centauri as it was 4.24 years ago. If it exploded tomorrow, we'd know nothing about it until the

light, and other forms of radiation, from the explosion reached us in 4.24 years time. So, Proxima Centauri is our nearest star, and more distant stars can be anything up to thousands or even millions of light years away. This means that we always receive out-of-date information about the Universe, which varies in age from one place to the next. A large amount of the information we receive dates from times long before humans even existed. The light from some galaxies was generated when dinosaurs still roamed the Earth. Looking into the Universe is like looking back in time.

WHAT DOES RADIATION FROM OUTER SPACE TELL US?

The advantage of detecting different forms of radiation is that it provides scientists with information such as temperature differences in space or on stars. For example, telescopes that can detect x-rays show us regions of stars that are giving out extreme heat. Telescopes that can detect ultraviolet light can show us where gas clouds have formed in the atmosphere around planets. We can gain clues about the chemicals

◀ The largest group of radio telescopes consists of 27 individual radio telescopes and is found in New Mexico, USA. Their data is combined to produce a single fine-detail image of the sky.

from which stars and other space objects are made, depending on the type of radiation they give out. Some objects only give out radio waves and would otherwise be invisible. Whole galaxies have been revealed by the detection of radio waves.

Background radiation is present throughout the Universe and is made of microwaves and infrared radiation (heat). Scientists think that this is left over from the 'Big Bang' which created the Universe. Measuring this helps **cosmologists** (scientists who study the formation of the Universe) estimate the age of the Universe. Scientists have even listened to this background radiation on a type of radio. A fraction of the crackle that you hear on an analogue radio is the sound of the Big Bang – this is like listening to the formation of the Universe. The Spitzer space telescope detects infrared radiation. Most infrared radiation cannot be observed from the ground because it is blocked by Earth's atmosphere. Therefore, NASA (National Aeronautics and Space Administration) decided to send Spitzer into orbit around Earth from Cape Canaveral in Florida, USA, in 2003. It is the largest infrared telescope ever launched into space. Large parts of space are filled with dust and clouds of gas, which makes it difficult to see what is beyond with a visible-light-detecting telescope. However, Spitzer can detect infrared radiation

▲ ▼ The image above is of a galaxy viewed with a visible-light-detecting telescope, and the one below is viewed through an infrared-light-detecting telescope. You can see how different parts of the galaxy stand out in each image.

through the clouds and has revealed stars being born, newly-forming planetary systems and small stars that are normally too dim to see. Spitzer will carry on working until around 2008.

HERSCHEL SPACE OBSERVATORY

In 2007, the ESA (European Space Agency) will launch the Herschel Space Observatory. This telescope also detects infrared radiation and will study the formation of early galaxies and the creation of stars. It will also take a closer look at the surfaces of comets, planets and moons. In 2011, NASA will launch an even newer infrared telescope – the James Webb Space Telescope. Amongst other goals, astronomers hope that this telescope will find out the shape of the Universe, discover how solar systems interact with each other, and make some sense of the mysterious dark matter (see page 15). The observations of these telescopes are expected to be spectacular.

▼ This is how our Milky Way galaxy is believed to look. We are located towards the end of one of its arms. Over half of all observable galaxies are spiral.

GALAXIES

A galaxy is an enormous group of stars, planets, gas, dust, dark matter and dark energy held together by gravity. The galaxy in which our Solar System sits is called the Milky Way. In some parts of the world, you can clearly see a wide band of stars across the sky. This is one edge of our galaxy and is also often referred to as the Milky Way. Astronomers think that our galaxy contains around 100 billion stars and is only one of millions of other galaxies across the Universe. Our Solar System is always on the move because it orbits the centre of the Milky Way galaxy every 220 million years. It sits roughly 25,000 light-years away from the centre of the galaxy. Galaxies come in different forms. All galaxies are slightly different from each other in shape and size, but the three main types are spiral, elliptical and irregular.

Sun

Spiral galaxies – These galaxies have arms that spiral out from a central bulge. Our own galaxy is thought to be a spiral, and our Solar System is placed towards the end of one of the arms.

Elliptical galaxies – These galaxies range from perfect to flattened spheres. They are brightest at the centre and then fade towards the edges. Elliptical galaxies rotate more slowly than spiral galaxies and some astronomers think that they do not rotate at all.

Irregular galaxies – These galaxies lack a defined shape. Some of them contain mostly blue stars and clouds of gas, others are made mostly of bright young stars with a lot of gas and dust. The Small Magellanic Cloud is an irregular galaxy.

▲ This is the Small Magellanic Cloud. Around three per cent of observable galaxies are irregular.

Three galaxies are visible from the Earth to the naked eye. In the Northern Hemisphere you can see the Andromeda galaxy, which is about two million light years from the Earth. In the Southern Hemisphere you can see the Large and Small Magellanic Clouds, which are about 160,000 light years, and 180,000 light years away from the Earth, respectively. These three galaxies look like fuzzy patches of sky, or large blurry stars to the naked eye.

◀ Around 10 per cent of the observable galaxies are elliptical.

GALAXY CRASH

Galaxies are not stationary, and occasionally two galaxies can drift so close to one another that the gravity of each changes the shape of the other. Galaxies can even crash into each other. When this happens with fast-moving galaxies, they pass through each other and emerge on the other side with little effect. When slow-moving galaxies collide, they can form one massive galaxy. Such collisions have resulted in spirals of stars that can extend for over 100,000 light years into space.

BLACK HOLES

At the centre of almost every galaxy, if not all galaxies, is a black hole. A black hole is the result of the death of a super giant star (see page 24). It is not a hole, but rather a region of space from which nothing can return. A black hole is a vast ball of matter that has so much gravity that it keeps the galaxy spinning like a giant wheel. It can be as much as a billion times as massive as our Sun. A black hole slowly consumes its solar systems as they draw nearer.

Black holes get their name from their appearance, as even light cannot escape the immense gravitational pull. Black holes make themselves invisible – black against a black background – but astronomers can detect them because of the effects they have on other space objects. For example, stars get pulled into orbit around them and appear to flash on and off as they move in front and behind the black holes. As a star gets closer to a black hole, it eventually passes a point called the 'event horizon'. At this point, the star appears to vanish and is eventually torn apart and added to the mass of the black hole.

▼ These two galaxies are crashing into each other.

PATTERNS IN THE UNIVERSE

Astronomers have gathered evidence that shows that the Universe is immense in size, but still has a structure. All of the stars and their solar systems are arranged into galaxies. Only a few galaxies exist by themselves. Some galaxies exist in pairs and orbit each other, but most are found in Groups. Relatively few galaxies exist by themselves. Groups typically contain less than 50 galaxies. Our galaxy is in a Local Group that contains over 30 galaxies. Larger groups of galaxies are called **clusters**. One cluster can contain between 50 and 1,000 galaxies and can have a diameter as large as 10 million light years. It would take billions and billions of years – an unimaginably long time– to travel from one side of a cluster to another.

Clusters of galaxies are grouped into even larger groups – **superclusters**. At the very largest scales of the visible Universe, all matter is gathered into wall-like structures that surround vast voids (empty spaces). This is the same kind of pattern as you see in foam, such as bubble bath. One of the wall-like structures is called the Great Wall and is a supercluster of galaxies. It is situated over 250 million light years from the Earth, and is more than 500 million light years long, 200 million light years wide, and 20 million light years thick.

Traditionally, astronomers discovered clusters and superclusters through the use of light-detecting telescopes. Today, they use infrared surveys to spot distant clusters because galaxies contained within them often emit a lot of infrared radiation. Also, astronomers carry out radio surveys. Few objects in our galaxy give off radio waves, which means that any radio waves that astronomers detect are likely to come from objects outside our galaxy. Clusters of galaxies also emit hot plasma (gas) which gives off x-rays. Astronomers search the sky with x-ray-detecting telescopes and have discovered clusters and superclusters in this way.

▼ The objects of the Universe are arranged into wall-like structures that surround voids.

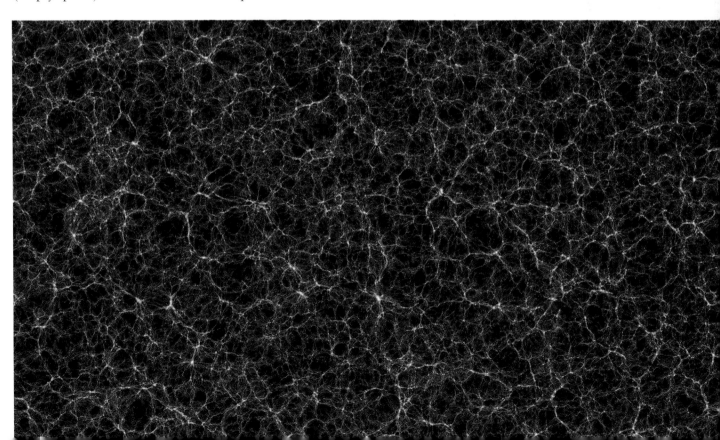

Cosmologists used to think that the Universe was in a fixed state – it was neither getting bigger nor smaller. In 1920, US astronomer, Vesto Slipher, discovered that galaxies were moving away from Earth, and that some galaxies were moving faster than others. In 1923, another US astronomer, Edwin Hubble, concluded that the Universe must be expanding, and should be thought of as a balloon being continually inflated.

At that time, other scientists thought that the Universe must be never ending. But if it were, surely the sky should be white at night instead of black because every part of the sky would be filled with the light from a star or galaxy? Hubble pointed out that other galaxies are probably travelling away from Earth so quickly that they disappear from view. So, this meant that the Universe could be never ending, but it also meant that it must be expanding from a central point.

In 1927, Belgian astronomer George Lemaitre described the Big Bang theory (that the Universe had begun with one enormous explosion, see page 14). US physicist Robert Dicke suggested it was more likely that the Universe first expands and then contracts over and over again, and that there have been an infinite number of Big Bangs already. If Dicke is correct, the expansion of the Universe should be slowing down, so that eventually it begins to contract. However, recent studies have shown that the Universe expansion is speeding up.

Another possibility, first put forward by three British astronomers in 1948, is that the Universe can create matter spontaneously from pockets of energy, which fill space as they expand. This idea is supported by the fact that there are still things that science can't fully explain, such as dark matter and dark energy.

Today, the most popular theory is that the Universe is expanding and will continue to do so for the whole of eternity. Cosmologists disagree over whether or not the Universe has an edge. Whichever theory proves to be correct, it takes an enormous leap of imagination from everyday thought to even begin to understand how the Universe might work.

◄ Edwin Hubble provided the first evidence for the Big Bang theory.

HOW BIG IS THE UNIVERSE?

Cosmologists do not know how big the Universe is, because with today's technology it is impossible to see far enough into outer space. However, cosmologists have calculated that the edge of the known, or observable, Universe is around 78 billion light years away. The actual Universe is likely to be greater in size than this, but no-one knows how much greater.

DOES THE UNIVERSE EVER END?

There are two ways that the Universe could 'end'. It could end in space, if it has an edge, or it could end in time, if there was actually a beginning or end of time. Both of these ideas are extremely difficult for humans to make sense of.

Speculation about how the Universe will end all depends on your point of view. According to the 'Big Bang' theory, the Universe will eventually stop expanding and begin to contract. It follows then, that the Universe will ultimately return to its original state – a very dense ball of matter that contains absolutely everything we call the Universe. This is called the '**Big Crunch**' theory. It may well be that everything then starts all over again, with another 'Big Bang'.

Based on other theories, the Universe may simply continue expanding forever, or it may stop expanding and stay as it is. The discovery of antimatter and black holes has led some scientists to suggest that there may also be a 'parallel universe' where everything is exactly the same but in reverse, like a mirror image. This other universe may balance our own in some way.

Other scientists believe that the Universe is infinite, which means that it has no beginning and no end. They also believe that the Universe exists infinitely in time, so that it has always existed in the past and will always exist in the future.

The truth is that scientists do not know enough about the Universe to comment with any certainty. That is why a number of different ideas remain in circulation instead of just one. That also means that you are free to make your own mind up too. Perhaps one day we'll discover enough about the Universe to understand its past, present and future.

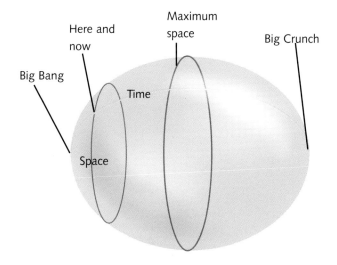

▲ The 'Big Bang' theory states that all space and time was created in one instant.

▲ The 'Big Crunch' theory states that all time and space will return to being a tiny and extremely dense ball.

IS THERE ANYTHING OUT THERE?

Scientists think that life on Earth may have begun when electricity, in the form of lightning, struck chemicals on Earth and turned them into amino acids. Amino acids are the basic building chemicals of life-forms. However, scientists have no idea whether this happened spontaneously on our planet, or whether basic organisms arrived from elsewhere. In 2005, a space probe called Deep Impact fired an 'impactor' (a smaller spacecraft) into a comet called Tempel 1. They hoped that the comet would give away some clues about the origins of life, as some scientists believe that a comet brought the first life to Earth.

CONDITIONS FOR LIFE

Life, as we know it, requires certain conditions to be able to thrive and evolve into the amazing variety of plants and animals on Earth today. Scientists believe that planets similar to Earth are few and far between across the galaxy and beyond. However, that does not rule out the possibility that simple life-forms, such as bacteria, exist in unlikely places, such as in the frozen waters of Mars, on Jupiter's moon Europa, or on comets.

WHAT HAVE SCIENTISTS FOUND?

Mars is covered with deep gorges that look as though they were carved out by water channels. Because of this, scientists think that rivers, lakes and seas once covered Mars, but that most of the water disappeared millions of years ago. In 2005, a space probe discovered a giant patch of frozen water on Mars, in a crater over 35 kilometres wide and up to two kilometres deep. Large lakes of water-ice are also present at Mars' poles, and possibly underneath its surface. The presence of water-ice suggests that Mars could have harboured life in the past, as water is a vital ingredient for life. In addition, it makes manned missions to Mars more possible as astronauts need accessible water in order to survive.

The Deep Impact experiment has given scientists a glimpse under the surface of the comet, which is likely to have remained unchanged since the Solar System formed. Scientists have masses of information to examine from this successful mission, and it is hoped that this project will answer basic questions about the formation of the Solar System, the composition of comets and whether a comet could have brought life to Earth.

▼ This photo, taken by the Viking 2 lander, shows the surface of Mars.

One of Jupiter's moons, Europa, is considered to be one of the most likely sites of life in our Solar System. It is an icy moon, but beneath the layer of ice, there may be an ocean of liquid water. On Earth, scientists have found vents of water, deep under the ocean, which support life. This discovery suggests that similar organisms might survive on Europa. Even if there is no longer an ocean on Europa, perhaps there was one in the past, which has left behind fossilised remains for future missions to uncover.

However, this is nowhere near a certainty as water is not the only necessary ingredient for life. For life to thrive there needs to be organic (carbon-containing) material and a continuous energy source.

ALIENS

Despite the unlikelihood of advanced life-forms living anywhere near Earth, it has not stopped people using their imaginations to invent extra-terrestrial life forms (aliens) in television and literature. In fiction, aliens have technologies and powers superior to our own, and can easily travel vast distances.

Such imagination demonstrates that humans have a very strong desire to explore the Universe and communicate with anything that might be out there. Because the Universe is so large, many people think that there has to be life elsewhere, but the

▶ Jupiter's moon Europa is one possible site of life in our Solar System.

distances involved between stars, solar systems and galaxies mean that it is a bit like an ant living in Britain, trying to find another ant living in America.

COMMUNICATION

Scientists take the search for extraterrestrial life very seriously. Not only do they look for signs of life in our Solar System, radio astronomers search for communication signals that might have been sent by beings in outer space. They also send communications signals into outer space to see whether anything will reply. Unfortunately, because of the distances involved, it could take a communication signal millions of years to be delivered and replied to.

◀ Science-fiction often portrays aliens with humanoid body shapes. If extraterrestrial life is found, it is unlikely to resemble humans in any way.

INVESTIGATE

▶ Look in library books or on the internet and find out what an organisation called S.E.T.I. is doing to try to find extraterrestrial life in the Universe. How many alien civilisations does S.E.T.I. estimate that there could be in our galaxy?

Glossary

ASTEROIDS – Small rocky bodies that revolve around the Sun. Asteroids are usually between a few and several hundred kilometres in diameter.

ASTRONOMERS – People whose area of research is astronomy (space science).

ATOMS – The basic smallest units that make up all substances in the Universe.

BIG BANG – A theory about the origin and evolution of our Universe. The theory states that the Universe began roughly 14 billion years ago as an extremely dense and incredibly hot ball. It then expanded rapidly to create everything in the Universe.

BIG CRUNCH – A theory about how the Universe may end. This theory states that the Universe will end by shrinking in on itself and returning to the same state as it started – an incredibly dense and hot ball of matter.

BLACK DWARF – The remains of a Sun-sized star which has changed into a white dwarf and then cooled down further to become a black dwarf.

CLUSTER – A group of galaxies which are affected by each others' gravitational pull. The term cluster can also refer to a small group of stars.

COMETS – Lumps of icy matter that orbit the Sun. They have two tails.

COSMOLOGISTS – Scientists who study the evolution of the Universe and the relationship between space and time in the Universe.

EVOLVE – Gradual development.

FAULT LINES – Cracks in the Earth's crust. They are found where two tectonic plates meet. Earthquakes are caused by the build-up of pressure as two plates move past each other.

FUSION – The process in which the nuclei of two atoms come together with such force that they join and become a heavier atom.

GALAXY – A huge collection of stars, gas and dust measuring many light years across, and held together by gravity. The Earth is located in the Milky Way galaxy.

ANSWERS

p15 Test yourself
Gravity is the force that holds everything onto the Earth's surface. If there was no gravity, you would float off into space. The force of gravity holds all the planets in orbit around the Sun. It also holds moons in orbit around the planets.

p21 Test yourself
A meteorite is a lump of matter that has fallen to the Earth's surface from space. A meteoroid is a lump of matter smaller than an asteroid that is moving through space. A meteor is a lump of matter that burns up as it passes into the Earth's atmosphere and shows up as a bright trail or streak in the night sky. Meteors are also called falling or shooting stars.

Asteroids are made of rocks and metals. Asteroids do not have any tails. Comets are made of ice, rock and carbon-based substances. Comets have two tails.

p25 Investigate
Two constellations that are easy to spot in the Northern Hemisphere are Orion and The Plough (also known as the Big Dipper), which is part of a larger constellation called Ursa Major. In the Southern Hemisphere, the Southern Cross is an easily identifiable constellation. It is made up of four stars in the shape of a cross and is also called the Crux.

p33 Test yourself
Mercury, Venus, Earth, Mars, Jupiter, Saturn, Uranus, Neptune and Pluto.

p45 Investigate
S.E.T.I. stands for Search for Extraterrestrial Intelligence. S.E.T.I. uses radio telescopes to search for signals from outer space. It conducts research in a number of fields including astronomy and planetary sciences, chemical evolution, the origins of life, biological and cultural evolution. S.E.T.I. estimates that there could be up to 100 million extraterrestrial civilisations in the Milky Way – or we could be alone.

GRAVITY – The pulling force of attraction between all bodies in the Universe. All objects exert a gravitational force. The larger an object, the greater its gravitational force.

LAVA – Magma that a volcano expels during a volcanic eruption. Volcanic eruptions happen along fault lines where the Earth's crust is weakest.

LIGHT YEAR – The distance that light can travel in one year. Light travels at 299,792,458 metres per second. At this speed it travels 9,460,000,000,000 kilometres in one year.

LITHOSPHERE – The solid, topmost part of the upper mantle of the Earth and the Earth's crust.

MAGMA – The molten rock found beneath the Earth's solid surface.

MASS – A measure of the amount of matter contained by an object.

METEOR – A fragment of rocky debris that burns as it passes into the Earth's atmosphere. Meteors are seen as bright trails or streaks in the night sky.

METEORITE – A fragment of rocky debris that is large enough not to have been completely burnt up in the Earth's atmosphere, and has therefore reached the Earth's surface.

METEOROID – A fragment of rocky debris moving through space. Meteoroids are smaller than asteroids.

MOLECULE – Two or more atoms joined together. For example, a water molecule is made up of two hydrogen atoms joined together with one oxygen atom.

NEBULA – A cloud of gas and/or dust in space. Planetary nebulae are shells of gas around a dead or dying star. A supernova can produce a nebula.

ORBIT – The path that one object takes around another, often under the influence of gravity. For example, the Moon orbits the Earth, and the Earth orbits the Sun.

RED GIANT – A very large, cool star that is in the last stages of its life. Our Sun will eventually become a red giant the size of the Earth's orbit.

SUPERCLUSTER – A vast collection of galaxy clusters. Superclusters may contain tens of thousands of galaxies and span over 100 million light-years of space. They are the largest known structures in the Universe.

SUPERNOVA – The explosion caused when an enormous star over eight times our Sun's mass dies and collapses. These explosions are very bright and can shine as brightly as an entire galaxy.

UNIVERSE – Everything that we know to exist. It includes all matter, energy, space and time. We do not know for certain how big the Universe is, whether it begins or ends, or how old it is.

WHITE DWARF – The remainder of a red giant star. White dwarfs are small and dense.

YELLOW DWARF – A relatively small star in the main sequence of its life.

Useful websites:
www.bbc.co.uk/schools
www.howstuffworks.com
www.newscientist.com
www.popsci.com
www.sciencenewsforkids.org

Index

Photo Credits – *(abbv: r, right, l, left, t, top, m, middle, b, bottom)* **Cover background image** NASA, ESA and A.Nota (STSCI/ESA) **Front cover images** (l) David Nunuk/Science Photo Library (r) Image courtesy of MODIS Rapid Response Project at NASA/GSFC **Back cover image** (inset) David Nunuk/Science Photo Library **p.1** (tr) NASA/JPL-Caltech/K. Gordon (University of Arizona) & S. Willner (Harvard-Smithsonian Center for Astrophysics) (bl) NASA, The Hubble Heritage Team, STScI, AURA, Amy Simon Cornell (br) NASA, Massimo Stiavelli, STScI ODButterfly Nebula **p.2** NASA/JPL-Caltech/R. Hurt (SSC) **p.3** (t) JPL (b) Bob Eggleton (www.bobeggleton.com) **p.4** (tl) David Rydevik (tr) NASA (bl) NASA (br) NASA **p.5** NASA, The Hubble Heritage Team, STScI, AURA **p.6** NASA **p.8** (t) Lloyd Cluff/CORBIS (b) David Rydevik **p.9** Reuters/CORBIS **p.10** Image courtesy of MODIS Rapid Response Project at NASA/GSFC **p.13** Richard Hamilton Smith/CORBIS **p.14** NASA **p.15** NASA and The Hubble Heritage Team (STScI/AURA) W. Blair (JHU) and D. Malin (David Malin Images) **p.16** NASA Apollo **p.18** Professor Jay Pasachoff/Science Photo Library **p.19** Dan Schechter/Science Photo Library **p.20** Tony & Daphne Hallas/Science Photo Library **p.20** NASA **p.21** (t) NASA (b) NASA Jet Propulsion Laboratory (NASA-JPL) **p.22** NASA **p.24** NASA, Massimo Stiavelli, STScI ODButterfly Nebula **p.25** (br) Douglas Kirkland/CORBIS **p.27** U.S. Geological Survey **p.28** (t) JPL (b) NASA, Steve Lee University of Colorado, Jim Bell Cornell University **p.29** NASA, The Hubble Heritage Team, STScI, AURA, Amy Simon Cornell **p.30** NASA/JPL/Space Science Institute **p.32** NASA **p.33** Bob Eggleton (www.bobeggleton.com) **p.34** Bettmann/CORBIS **p.35** (t) Jim Sugar/CORBIS (b) Fermilab/Science Photo Library **p.36** David Nunuk/Science Photo Library **p.37** (t) N.A. Sharp (NOAO/AURA/NSF) (b) NASA/JPL-Caltech/K. Gordon (University of Arizona) & S. Willner (Harvard-Smithsonian Center for Astrophysics) **p.38** NASA/JPL-Caltech/R. Hurt (SSC) **p.39** (t) NASA, ESA and A.Nota (STSCI/ESA) (b) NASA, Thomas M. Brown Charles W. Bowers Randy A. Kimble, Allen V. **p.40** NASA, The Hubble Heritage Team, STScI, AURA **p.41** Image courtesy of the Virgo Consortium. **p.42** Emilio Segre Visual Archives/American Institute of Physics/Science Photo Library **p.44** NASA **p.45** (t) NASA